NATIVITY SET

ALSO BY ROBERT HUDSON

The Christian Writer's Manual of Style, 5th Edition

The Beautiful Madness of Martin Bonham:
A Tale about Loving God

Kiss the Earth When You Pray:
The Father Zosima Poems

The Further Adventures of Jack the Giant Killer

Seeing Jesus: Visionary Encounters
from the First Century to the Present

The Art of the Almost Said:
A Christian Writer's Guide to Writing Poetry

The Poet and the Fly: Art, Nature, God,
Mortality, and Other Elusive Mysteries

The Monk's Record Player:
Thomas Merton, Bob Dylan, and the Perilous Summer of 1966

Rondels for After:
Translations of Poems by Tristan Corbière (chapbook)

Bugs: A Haiku Anthology

Making a Poetry Chapbook (chapbook)

NATIVITY SET

Table-Top Meditations for Christmas

Poems by ROBERT HUDSON
Illustrations by MARK SHEERES

Apocryphile Press
PO Box 255
Hannacroix, NY 12087
www.apocryphilepress.com

Copyright © 2025 by Robert Hudson
Printed in the United States of America
ISBN 978-1-965646-49-6 | paper
ISBN 978-1-965646-50-2 | epub

Please join our mailing list at www.apocryphilepress.com/free. We'll keep you up-to-date on all our new releases, and we'll also send you a FREE BOOK. Visit us today!

CONTENTS

PART TWO: THE STORY OF THE CRÈCHE

INTRODUCTION

The poetic form called the "rondel" was devised by thirteenth-century French troubadours, the popular poet-musicians of the time, as a way of exploring new ideas and new modes of expression. The form has since been adapted by English poets as diverse as Chaucer, Robert Louis Stevenson, and Marilyn Hacker.

Not coincidentally, Francis of Assisi devised the crèche scene at about that same time. As a youth he had traveled to France on family business, and it was there that he fell in love with the songs and poems of the troubadours. Although christened Giovanni at birth, he acquired the name Francis due to his love for all things French. Eventually, fired by the troubadours' creativity, he wrote his own songs and poems, though with deeply religious themes, like his beautiful "Canticle of the Sun," and in time he came to be known as "the troubadour of God." Whether he was aware of the rondel form is unknown, but like the troubadours he sought to explore new ideas and new modes of expression. The crèche scene was one of his most inspired. (See "Part Two: The Story of the Crèche" for more detail.)

The rondels in the following collection use the original French form of thirteen lines, with its repeating refrains and limited rhymes, and a sonnet serves as the prologue.

My prayer is that these poem-meditations might be a blessing to you and your family year after year—perhaps even while you set up the figurines of your own nativity set.

Robert Hudson
Epiphany 2025

NATIVITY SET

PART ONE:
MEDITATIONS

PROLOGUE: PREPARING FOR CHRISTMAS

the angel, shepherd, lamb, and stable
the magi, Joseph, Child, and Mary
I set them gently on the table
a sort of wordless lectionary

amid the festive reds and greens
of Santas, trees, and celebration
my hope is that these figurines
may be an aid to contemplation

so listen closely to the crèche
to what each figure has to say
that they might help us see afresh
the miracle of Christmas day

for all the world gathers here
to see Who's born again this year

If there be any virtue, and if there be any praise,
think on these things (Philippians 4:8)

STAR

a radiant star hangs from a nail
in clouds of faded angel hair
and drops its gilding here and there
in flecks of white and yellow hail

the zigzag of the comet trail
outlines a fiery golden stair
a radiant star hangs from a nail
in clouds of faded angel hair

its jagged glow will never fail
to testify through light and air
how Jesus born beneath its glare
against sharp iron would prevail

a radiant Star hangs from a nail

The star, which they saw in the east, went before them,
till it came and stood over where the young child was (Matthew 2:9)

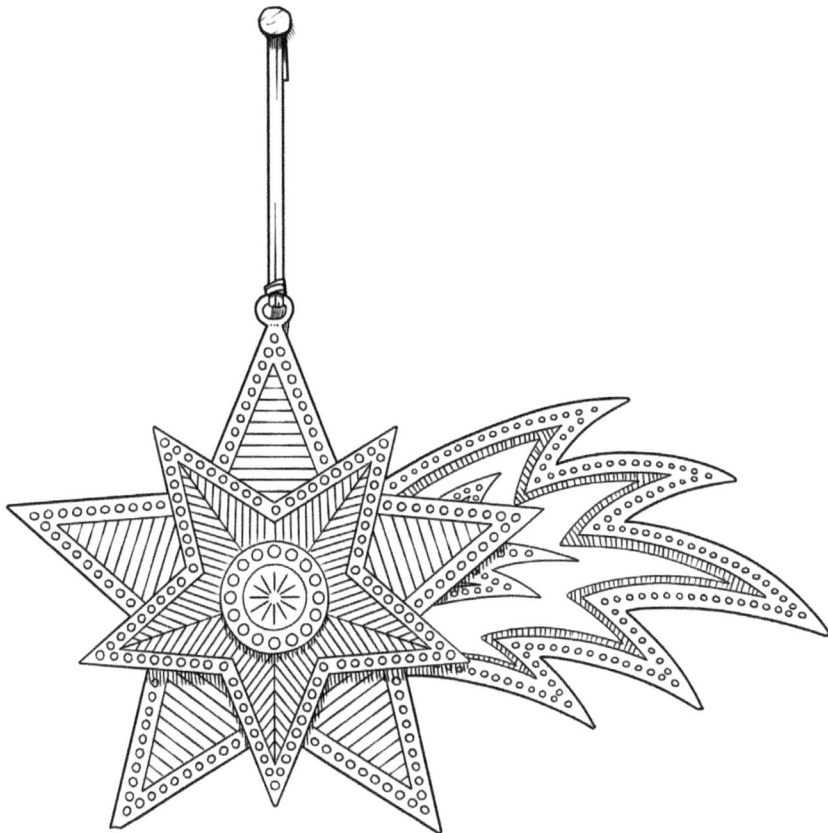

4

MAGI

these gentlemen have dignity
though long in storage they have been
each little wooden manikin
is draped in paint and finery

though one is stooped upon his knee
another chipped in hand and chin
these gentlemen have dignity
though long in storage they have been

for they have journeyed far to see
the place where Love puts on a skin
at every footstep trusting in
its distant possibility

these gentlemen have dignity

And when they were come into the house,
they saw the young child with Mary his mother,
and fell down, and worshipped him (Matthew 2:11)

GIFTS

a rustic box contains all three
the myrrh and frankincense and gold
though it seems curiously bold
to offer pelf and potpourri

to One still in His infancy
and lying in a dank sheepfold
a rustic box contains all three
the myrrh and frankincense and gold

but here's a rare epiphany
almost as if it were foretold
that like those offerings threefold
this manger holds a Trinity

a rustic box contains all Three

They presented unto him gifts;
gold, and frankincense and myrrh (Matthew 2:11)

CAMEL

how vast the distances he's crossed
this ragged camel rough as bark
(we borrowed him from Noah's ark
when our original got lost)

enduring rain and sun and frost
and ponderous loads without remark
how vast the distances he's crossed
this ragged camel rough as bark

but all his burdens can't exhaust
the joy he feels to see that Spark
enkindling hope within the dark
for all who wander tempest-tossed

how vast the distances He's crossed

The people that walked in darkness have seen a great light:
they that dwell in the land of the shadow of death,
upon them hath the light shined (Isaiah 9:2)

OLD SHEPHERD

the shepherd leaning on his staff
commands no other retinue
than one old goat, a lamb, a ewe,
a ram with broken horns, a calf

the magi do not dare to laugh
since camels have worn ragged too
the shepherd leaning on his staff
commands no other retinue

his shepherd's crook once broke in half
now wears a little ring of glue
for Love that makes the broken new
will break itself on his behalf

the shepherd leaning on his staff

There were in the same country shepherds abiding in the field,
keeping watch over their flock by night (Luke 2:8)

II

12

ANGEL

this angel has a tale to tell
a wondrous message to convey
and in her firm but gentle way
above the fields of Israel

she speaks to shepherd boys, as well
as to each one of us today
this angel has a tale to tell
a wondrous message to convey

not even mighty Gabriel
could find a better way to say
"for unto you is born this day
a Savior, Christ, Emmanuel"

this angel has a tale to tell

I bring you good tidings of great joy, which shall be to all people.
For unto you is born this day in the city of David a Savior,
which is Christ the Lord (Luke 2:10–11)

YOUNG SHEPHERD

bright angels hovering around
resplendent in the midnight sky
enthralled the youngest shepherd's eye
and nearly struck him to the ground

with how their voices did resound
"all glory to our God most high"
bright angels hovering around
resplendent in the midnight sky

but at the stable door he found
that dazzled looks, a muted cry
were all he had to testify
to that vast staggering sight and sound

bright angels hovering around

Suddenly there was with the angel a multitude
of the heavenly host praising God, and saying,
"Glory to God in the highest, and on earth peace,
good will toward men" (Luke 2:13–14)

LAMB

as it was written in the Word
"the wolf beside the lamb shall dwell"
but should we throw a wolf pell-mell
into this tranquil stable's herd?

the shepherd boy has surely heard
"a branch shall grow in Israel"
as it was written in the Word
"the wolf beside the lamb shall dwell"

so maybe it's not too absurd
on this most sacred first Noel
to welcome brother wolf as well
the newborn Lamb seems undeterred

as it was written in the Word

There shall come forth a rod out of the stem of Jesse,
and a Branch shall grow out of his roots:
… The wolf also shall dwell with the lamb (Isaiah 11:1, 6)

OX AND ASS

the ox and ass are at the door
with eyes turned dimly toward the face
of someone sleeping in their place
who occupies the stable floor

the painted eyes see little more
than unfamiliar populace
the ox and ass are at the door
with eyes turned dimly toward the face

but in their way they too adore
while standing dumbly on their base
and sense an odd unearthly Grace
with something untamed at its core

the ox and ass are at the door

Thou shalt not muzzle the mouth of the ox that treadeth out the corn.
Doth God take care for oxen? (1 Corinthians 9:9)

20

ROOSTER

his presence is a mystery
this rooster we call Chanticleer
no one recalls how he got here
and joined our grave nativity

but as our feathered adoptee
he swaggers in year after year
his presence is a mystery
this rooster we call Chanticleer

because he crows at dawn maybe
it is the Child he's come to hear
whose cries will cause there to appear
a strange new day in Galilee

His presence is a mystery

Take heed, as unto a light that shineth in a dark place,
until the day dawn, and the day star arise in your hearts (2 Peter 1:19)

STABLE

to frame the splendor of this scene
four wooden slats are cut off square
to house the stately disrepair
of each adoring figurine

dried lichen stuck into a screen
forms this nativity's parterre
to frame the splendor of this scene
four wooden slats are cut off square

but what do wooden stables mean
by sheltering such pieces there
if not to say that this is where
the fragments of the world convene

to frame the splendor of this scene

Mine eyes have seen thy salvation, which thou
hast prepared before the face of all people (Luke 2:30–31)

MARY AND JOSEPH

the stillness centered in the mind
absorbs this woman and this man
who do not turn around to scan
the ragged tokens of mankind

the teeming nations here combined
in swain and Ethiopian
the stillness centered in the mind
absorbs this woman and this man

they kneel in silence wholly blind
to everything but Love's clear plan
they do not blink or move nor can
they sense the golden disk behind

the stillness centered in the mind

All they that heard it wondered at those things
which were told them by the shepherds.
But Mary kept all these things, and
pondered them in her heart (Luke 2:18–19)

MANGER

a wooden X at either end
and in between the straw is spread
but this is not a crib or bed
from which the child's arms unbend

it is a hollow trough that fed
the ass and ox where they were penned
a wooden X at either end
and in between the straw is spread

can any of them comprehend
why even distant stars are led
to worship in this cattle shed
the One whose life must yet transcend

a wooden X at either end

*This shall be a sign unto you; Ye shall find the babe
wrapped in swaddling clothes, lying in a manger (Luke 2:12)*

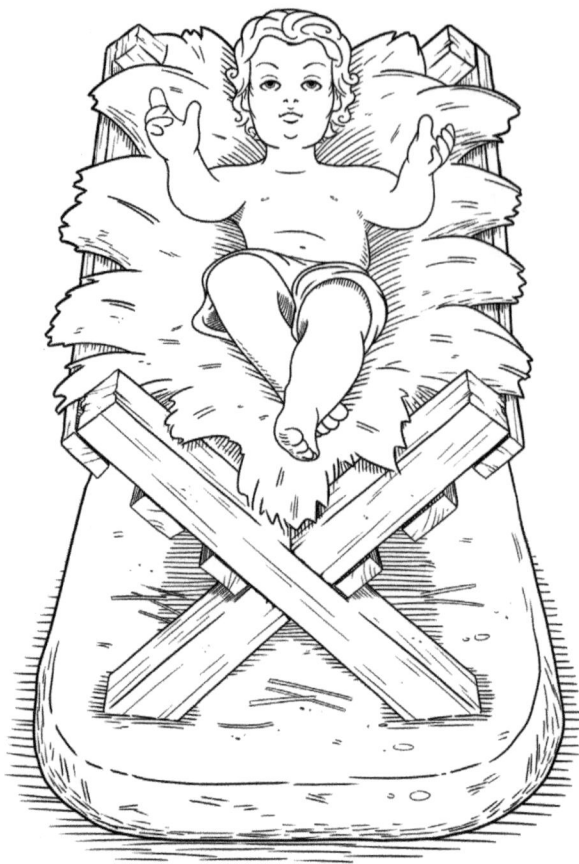

CHILD

but only when the Child appears
is this nativity made whole
the star may drift from pole to pole
the shepherd boy may wait for years

the ass and ox may twitch their ears
as magi stumble toward their goal
but only when the Child appears
is this nativity made whole

and we who wrestle with our fears
whose sin and sorrow take their toll
we long to hear within our soul
the song of Grace that Mary hears

but only when the Child appears

The time is fulfilled, and the kingdom of God is at hand:
repent ye, and believe the gospel (Mark 1:15)

HE IS

He is the Shepherd of the fold
He is the Star of Bethlehem
He is the magi's diadem
He is the gift of lustrous gold

He is the One who was foretold
He is the shoot of Jesse's stem
He is the Shepherd of the fold
He is the Star of Bethlehem

He is the shelter from the cold
He is the heir of Abraham
He is the sacrificial Lamb
He is the wonder we behold

He is the Shepherd of the fold

I am the good shepherd: the good shepherd
giveth his life for the sheep (John 10:11)

31

EPILOGUE: KEEPING CHRISTMAS

to keep them safe another year
we lay them neatly in the box
the Child, the star, the ass and ox,
the holy parents drawing near

and even strutting Chanticleer
among the shepherds' meager flocks
to keep them safe another year
we lay them neatly in the box

and wait for Christ to reappear
with all the mysteries He unlocks
like this most holy paradox
we await the One who's always here

to keep Him safe another year

For we are saved by hope: but hope that is seen is not hope:
for what a man seeth, why doth he yet hope for? (Romans 8:24)

PART TWO:
THE STORY OF THE CRÈCHE

THE STORY OF THE CRÈCHE: A BRIEF HISTORY

SAINT FRANCIS

According to tradition, we have Francis of Assisi to thank for the crèche. His official biographer, Bonaventure, wrote that in 1223, while on a journey from Assisi to Naples at Christmastime, Francis "was minded, at the town of Greccio, to celebrate the memory of the Birth of the Child Jesus, with all the added solemnity that he might, for the kindling of devotion."[1] So Francis found a manger—an animal's feeding trough—and brought it to a cave not far from the local church. He lined it with hay and had an ass and ox brought in to add verisimilitude to the scene. The cave, he must have felt, was unusually appropriate because two years earlier he had visited the Holy Land and seen the "grotto of the nativity," a similar cave beneath the Church of the Nativity in Bethlehem, thought by some to be the site of Jesus's birth.

Francis's innovative worship resulted in an extraordinarily festive Christmas for the people of Greccio—which is to say, an extraordinarily festive Christ Mass. As Bonaventure wrote, "The folk assembled, the wood echoed with their voices, and that august night was made radiant and solemn with many bright lights, and with tuneful and sonorous praises. The man of God, filled with tender love, stood before the manger, bathed in tears, and overflowing with joy."[2]

While Francis preached to the crowd that day, one of his local followers, a knight by the name of John of Greccio, received a sudden and overpowering vision. He seemed to see the infant Jesus asleep in the manger, but when Francis leaned over to pick him up, the child awoke "when the blessed Father Francis embraced him in both arms."[3] Several miracles ensued, and even the hay from that manger was later said to have healing powers.

Insofar as Francis used live animals, what he presented was a living nativity—a variation on the traditional crèche scene that is still practiced among churches today at their Christmas pageants, though such presentations predated Francis by many centuries. Christians in the third and fourth centuries created tableaux in which people would stand as still as statues to present a scene—a sort of static drama of a kind that even the Romans had staged earlier as part of their theatrical pagan ceremonies.

Despite John of Greccio's vision, the manger in Francis's spare tableau was empty. No child. This was a drama of expectation in which the world awaited the appearance of the Messiah as foretold in Isaiah: "The Lord himself shall give you a sign; Behold, a virgin shall conceive, and bear a son, and shall call his name Immanuel" (Isaiah 7:14). Francis's concept was a celebration of Advent as much as an anticipation of Christmas day.

PRESEPIO

Things might have ended there if Francis's simple worship service had not been commemorated in paintings by Giotto and others, depicting Francis gently placing John of Greccio's visionary infant in the manger; and not long after that, a vibrant nativity scene tradition evolved in Italy, called the presepio (from a Latin word meaning "crib"). Large, often nearly life-size, presepio figures, sculpted in stone or wood, would portray the key actors from the biblical story, and they were displayed in churches throughout Advent, usually from the Feast of the Immaculate Conception on December 8 to Epiphany on January 6.

In time, Franciscan monks began making small nativity figurines out of flour, salt, and water, a primitive form of plaster, which were called santibelli, "beautiful saints," which in turn inspired Italian craftspeople, especially in towns like Naples, to begin carving miniature nativity scenes in wood for laypeople's private devotions. It reached its great blossoming in the seventeenth century, which is why so many of our modern crèche figures, based on those Neapolitan models, are still garbed in late Renaissance peasants' clothing.

SANTONS

The Italian tradition spread north and west throughout Europe and especially to Provence, the southeastern part of France, where the santibelli became particularly popular. In the early years of the nineteenth century, a sculptor in Marseille named Jean-Louis Lagnel conceived the idea of adapting the Italian crèche tradition by molding terracotta nativity figures and painting them by hand, and soon Marseille became the center of one of the richest crèche traditions in the world, one that continues to this day.

These figures are called santons ("saints"), and they represent not just those present at the birth of Jesus but local Marseillais as well: the mayor, shopkeepers, women carrying baskets and jugs, street vendors, and, naturally, village musicians, because Lagnel had a special love for music. Most of his figures wore the colorful folk costumes of early nineteenth-century French men and women of the Midi. Artists in Marseille still produce these figures, and tourists can visit a museum dedicated to the Marseilles tradition—the Lagnel Museum, or Musée du Santon.

One of my favorite santons is the ravi, the "enraptured one." This character, dressed in ragged clothes, stands apart from the main drama, pointing to the sky. He is the town fool, or fada, and in some versions of the story he was the first to see the host of angels assembling in the sky to deliver the message, "Unto you is born this day in the city of David a Saviour, which is Christ the Lord" (Luke 2:11). But when the enraptured fada runs back to town to proclaim the good news, the people just laugh and ignore him. He's a fool, after all. Yet the lesson is poignant. Fool or not, he was the most perceptive and enthusiastic one of all, the living embodiment of Paul's words in 1 Corinthians 4:9–10: "We have been made a spectacle to the whole universe, to angels as well as to human beings. We are fools for Christ."

PUTZ

While the Italian presepio spread to other Catholic countries throughout Europe in various forms during the seventeenth and eighteenth centuries, it was often scorned by Protestant sects who viewed such scenes as exactly the kind of "graven images" prohibited by the third commandment (Exodus 20:4–6).

English dissenting groups like the Baptists, Anabaptists, Quakers, Puritans, and even some Methodists rigorously discouraged artistic representations in general and sculptures in particular, which explains why Protestant churches even to this day rarely display crosses with the crucified Jesus on them, unlike the Roman Catholic crucifix.

A slow transformation began in the eighteenth century, due in part to the mission-oriented Moravians, then under the leadership of Count Nikolaus Zinzendorf, who spread their ardent style of Christian worship throughout Europe, especially in England, Germany, and the Americas. Zinzendorf, unlike the Dissenters, believed that artistic representations of Jesus provided a powerfully emotive means of meditating on Jesus's death and resurrection, and he encouraged the faithful to study European religious painting and sculpture, while he himself commissioned the creation of fresh new works of art.

By the early nineteenth century, the Moravians had developed their own nativity scene tradition, called the putz (rhymes with *puts*, as in "he puts the putz in the parlor"), meaning "decoration." These were not just small nativity scenes; they could also be expanded into elaborate, detailed landscape dioramas, sometimes large enough to fill a room. The infant Jesus, of course, often illuminated by a candle, was always the central focus, but along with Mary, Joseph, the magi, and the shepherds, other relevant biblical characters could be found. Sometimes, off to one side, Isaiah the prophet might be represented to remind the faithful of his prophecy of the birth of Christ (Isaiah 7:14). In various corners of the presentation, you might find figures enacting the annunciation (Luke 1:26–38), Mary's visit to Elizabeth (Luke 1:39–45), the journey to Bethlehem (Luke 2:1–5), the presentation in the temple (Luke 2:22–40), the flight into Egypt (Matthew

2:13–14), and even the baptism of Jesus in the Jordan (Matthew 3:13–17). They became comprehensive visual recitations of the Christmas story, from ancient prophecies to the gospel narratives, or as I say in the prologue to this collection, "a sort of wordless lectionary."

In time the putz began to incorporate other peripheral pieces, animal figurines, festive fruits, sprigs of evergreen, and small devotional items. As each family assembled its own putz, a common social custom developed in which you would invite others to view your family's creation and talk about the meaning of each element, and then in turn you would be invited to view theirs.

Sometimes, as in the santos tradition, entire villages were presented. My wife and I live in the historic village of Old Salem, North Carolina, which is a living museum dedicated to the early Moravian settlers of Appalachia. Every December the local Moravian congregation displays an entire room-sized putz of the village itself as part of what they call their annual Candle Tea. It is stunning, and it, along with the famous Moravian lovefeast, has become an annual tradition for Christians of many denominations from all parts of the region.

One further Moravian innovation was the addition to the nativity scene, nearly two centuries ago, of the Moravian star. Many standard sets don't even include a Bethlehem star, or if they do, it's often a six-pointed Star of David in lieu of the five-pointed pentagram, which to many people suggests wizardry and magic. But the Moravians devised a geometrically complex twenty-six-pointed star that has become a virtual symbol of the Moravian church itself. Some such stars have as many as thirty-two, fifty, or even a hundred and ten points, and they symbolize not just the Star of Bethlehem but the illumination that Christ brings into the world.

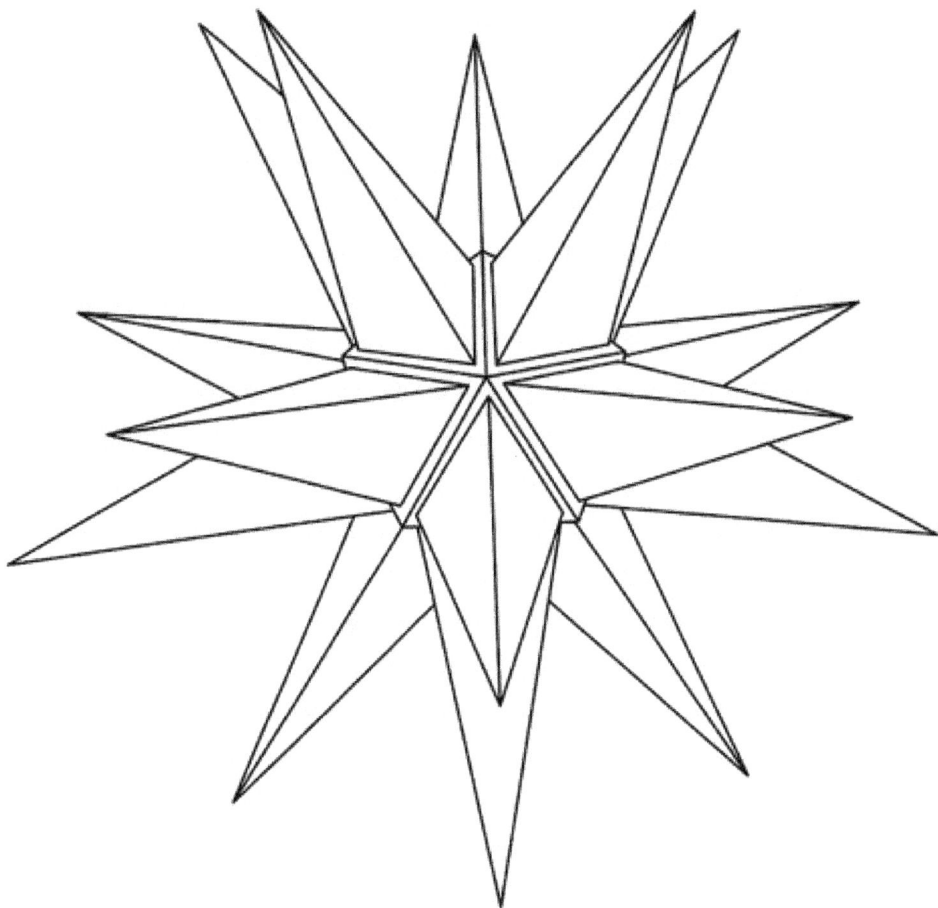

MODERN CRÈCHES

No era in history has seen more crèche sets available than ours. As early as Halloween, gift shops and online sellers begin offering a wide variety of sets from around the world—from the artistically sublime to the absurdly ridiculous. Once the seventeenth-century Italians introduced nativity characters in the garb of the Renaissance peasantry, the door was thrown wide open to all sorts of reinterpretations, from the santons of Provence to the whimsical modern sets consisting of dogs, cats, pigs, geese, mice, and moose, as well as sets with characters from *Star Wars*, superhero comics, *Frankenstein*, and zombie movies. Yes, a zombie crèche. You can find a nativity figure of Santa Claus kneeling beside the manger and one of Mary and Joseph taking selfies with the baby. Search the internet and you'll find photographs of sets made from cheese, peanuts, hotdogs, and balloons. It's difficult even to conceive of a bizarre crèche set that hasn't already been thought of, though I've yet to find one that portrays the characters as darkish-skinned Jewish Middle Easterners of the first century.

As an example of the bizarre: I once, somewhat impiously, added a *Where's Waldo?* figurine to our family's nativity set when I saw he was exactly the right scale—"Why, there's Waldo, right behind the magi!" Even my young daughters knew it was inappropriate—though I suppose I could have argued that he was a sort of an enraptured fool character from the santos tradition. But no. Waldo disappeared, and we now must search for him elsewhere.

Still, in a strange way, a bit of quirkiness is the point of a crèche—to animate our imaginations because, after all, even the most traditional scenes are only imaginative re-creations, dubious at best. The details are largely inaccurate and anachronistic, from the Italian clothing to a pristine, fair-skinned Mary in a blue robe. There were no little drummer boys in Bethlehem or bag-piping shepherds, no haloes encircling heads or angels holding unfurled banners that read, "Gloria in excelsis Deo." In fact, unlike most of the angels portrayed in the average crèche set, not a single female angel appears anywhere in the Bible. And we don't know what the star really was—a comet, a supernova, a planetary conjunction, an astral occultation? And who exactly were the magi and how many were there? Scholars disagree. Was the site of Jesus's birth a stable, a cave, a house? Debate continues.

But the crèche transcends all such debates because it is a symbolic and poetic presentation of truths that are deeper than the scanty documented facts, truth made palpable not just to our time and place but to all times and places. It opens us to a kind of inner vision of how the scene might have taken place and speaks to our hearts rather than our minds, forcing us to use our imaginations to grasp the significance of those almost unimaginably momentous events. As Sir Thomas Browne wrote, "Where I cannot satisfy my reason, I love to humor my fancy."[4] And one way of humoring one's fancy about the crèche, I believe, is to write poems.

MODERN MAKERS

It is precisely this risk of being ridiculous that can sometimes lead to the beautifully sublime in such creations as those of German woodworkers, who are world famous for their exquisite nativity sets, finely carved and hand painted. Such workshops as ALBL Oberammergau, Sievers-Hahn, Walter Werner, and Hummel produce exquisite figurines that have stood the test of time as works of art in themselves and often command high prices on the collector's market.

As you might expect, Italy produces some of the finest and most gorgeous nativity sets available. The Heide company of Pontives, Italy, makes ultra-detailed, realistic figures in very natural poses, quite unlike the stagey poses of many nativity figures. The woodworkers at companies like Anri and ULPE produce beautiful hand-carved, hand-painted figurines; the artists at the Sofia company make exquisite ceramic nativity scenes; and the Fontanini company of Bagni di Lucca makes graceful, Renaissance-style resin figures that are economical and widely available in North America.

My wife and I have cherished our Fontanini set since our children were small; it became a rich part of our family's Christmas tradition. We collected their four-and-a-half-inch-size pieces, which are no longer produced, but the company still makes nearly identical five-inch-size pieces that are some of the most popular crèche figures in the world. Fontanini makes figurines in sizes from a delicate three-and-a-half inches to a massive four feet, which harks back to the Franciscan santibelli, suitable for display in church chancels. Their sets include different versions of each of the traditional characters—several poses for Mary, Joseph, the magi, and so on—as well as such miscellaneous figures as carpenters, farmers, washerwomen, cooks, musicians, vendors, solitary wanderers, a wide variety of animals, and even a little drummer boy ("Pa rum pum pum pum"!).

The rooster in my rondel, of course, is not a part of the traditional nativity set, but the symbolism of the dawning of a new day is just too relevant to ignore. Not only does our set have a splendid rooster but also various chickens, ducks, geese, a quail, a pheasant, a turkey, as well as a couple of lively goose girls.

CHILDREN

All of which underscores the fact that nativity sets are for children. The traditional szopki ("crèche") nativity sets of Poland, for instance, often include moving puppets, and in Germany, the tradition is to wait until Christmas morning before placing the infant Jesus in the manger—as a way of heightening both the symbolism and the drama for the children in the house.

Children naturally identify with the baby in the manger—and with the animals as well, as William Blake understood when he wrote his poem "The Lamb":

> He is meek & he is mild,
> He became a little child:
> I a child & thou a lamb,
> We are callèd by his name.[5]

The presence of lambs, sheep, oxen, donkeys, fowl, and camels (both one- and two-hump!) makes the crèche especially exciting for children, nearly on a par with play sets of Noah's ark. (I've even seen a nativity set in which one of the magi arrives on an elephant!) The barnyard animals that surround the Christ child are so closely identified with his birth that it almost seems as though God were bestowing a blessing on the entire animal kingdom. They too have been included to share in this most miraculous event.

Children have a way of relishing, living in, and even creating miniature worlds. Dolls can take on imaginary personalities and Lego sets can recount epic stories. Children imagine scaling mountains made of crumpled blankets and sailing toy boats across the ocean of the living-room carpet. In that way, children reduce life's unmanageable mysteries—both the enchanting and the terrifying—to manageable proportions. So with the nativity set, the scene becomes the child's world.

What greater mystery could there be than the story of the One who sustains the vast, unfathomable universe becoming human—a tiny infant nonetheless?

A crèche set not only poses that profound question to us and to our children, but it begins to provide an answer as well.

A FINAL WORD

Our crèche includes a figure holding up a lantern and peering at something—surprised, alarmed, curious? I'm not sure. He looks a bit like how I imagine Diogenes, the ancient Greek cynic philosopher, must have looked when he held a lantern up to people's faces in broad daylight and exclaimed that he was searching for an "honest man." But this figure is clearly not Diogenes (though the search for honest men continues in our time).

For some crèche makers, the lantern bearer is Joseph because according to legend the radiance of the newborn Jesus himself outshone the lantern that Joseph held up to aid the midwives at their work. Others suggest that this figure is one of the shepherds, perhaps half-blinded by the angels' magnificent aerial display, who has gone in search of the newborn Savior in the darkened streets of Bethlehem. Still others say this character is the innkeeper who turned the weary, expectant couple away from the inn.

For our nativity set, the latter suggestion seems the most probable. The figurine seems more bemused than Joseph would have been, and he does not wear the clothing of a rustic shepherd; he is more well-to-do. So innkeeper he must be.

But further, the symbolism embodied by the innkeeper is perfect. He represents anyone who might turn Christ from the door, or as a minister friend of mine says, at some point everyone, whether or not they become believers, has to wrestle with "the Jesus thing"—Who was he? What was his message? What do his teachings mean? In short, we all must choose whether we have room for him or not. In this way, we too become part of the scene. With an inner lantern, we can be either deniers or seekers.

With all that in mind, I had a thought. We usually keep our nativity set on the closed lid of the piano, but what if the piano some year were to become too cluttered with other Christmas bric-a-brac? Although imaginary, this possibility inspired one final rondel.

INNKEEPER

no room for the nativity
since all the surfaces are packed
with every Christmas artifact
and myriad Yuletide filigree

and so my figurines must flee
to somewhere else not as compact
no room for the nativity
since all the surfaces are packed

so I set them up beneath the tree
a sad but necessary act
which leads to this ironic fact
this year the innkeeper is me

no room for the nativity

ACKNOWLEDGMENTS

Seven of these poems were published in *The Mennonite* in 2002. The rest were written in the past two years, though this book would never have been completed without the help of the following people. Thank you to

- Shelley Townsend-Hudson for encouraging me not to give up on this project.
- Mark Sheeres for all his beautiful artwork through the years.
- Rev. Dr. John Mabry of Apocryphile Press for his visionary, cutting-edge publishing.
- Janeen Jones for her meticulous proofreading.
- Tim Beals of Credo Communications and Rev. Virginia Tobiassen of Home Moravian Church, Winston-Salem, NC, for encouraging me to expand this collection beyond the original seven poems.
- For their kind endorsements, a special thanks to Ann Spangler and Tania Runyan.
- Sally Gant for lending me her books about Moravian Christmas traditions.

NOTES

1. Bonaventure, *The Life of Saint Francis*, trans. Emma Gurney Salter (J. M. Dent, 1932), 110–11. Francis of Assisi was born in 1181 and died in 1226. Bonaventure (1221–1274), a second-generation Franciscan, wrote his Life of Saint Francis between 1260 and 1263.

2. *Life of Saint Francis*, 111.

3. *Life of Saint Francis*, 111.

4. Thomas Browne, *Religio Medici* (Dent, 1896), 13.

5. William Blake, "The Lamb," *Songs of Innocence and of Experience* (The William Blake Trust/Princeton University Press, 1998), 38.

About the
Author & Illustrator

ROBERT HUDSON was a book editor at Zondervan for thirty-four years. He is the author of *The Christian Writer's Manual of Style* and other books, including *The Beautiful Madness of Martin Bonham, Kiss the Earth When You Pray, Seeing Jesus, The Poet and the Fly,* and *The Further Adventures of Jack the Giant Killer.* He is a member of the Chrysostom Society.

MARK SHEERES has been drawing and creating art in one form or another for as many years as he can remember. He has been designing, laying out, and illustrating books professionally since 2002. Among his other projects, he has illustrated Robert Hudson's *Further Adventures of Jack the Giant Killer* and *Kiss the Earth When You Pray.*

www.ingramcontent.com/pod-product-compliance
Lightning Source LLC
LaVergne TN
LVHW070058080426

835510LV00027B/3434